Sugarflood

poems

Mike Santora

Finishing Line Press
Georgetown, Kentucky

Sugarflood

For my mother

Copyright © 2017 by Mike Santora
ISBN 978-1-63534-283-3 First Edition
All rights reserved under International and Pan-American Copyright Conventions. No part of this book may be reproduced in any manner whatsoever without written permission from the publisher, except in the case of brief quotations embodied in critical articles and reviews.

ACKNOWLEDGMENTS

My deepest gratitude to everyone who helped make this chapbook possible. For their encouragement and tireless support, thank you to my family and friends. For their careful reading and creative guidance, thank you to Alex Ledford, Jayce Russell, Noah Burton, and John Vesey. To my teachers, David Rivard, Charles Simic, and Mekeel McBride. A special thanks to my *Sugarflood* production team, Miles Budimir, John Mengerink, John Hansel, and Allison Washko. Of course, Uncle Boo and Cousin Al. And most importantly, thank you to my wife, Christine, and my sweet bug, Julia Jazz.

Publisher: Leah Maines

Editor: Christen Kincaid

Cover Art: John Mengerink

Author Photo: John Hansel

Cover Design: Elizabeth Maines McCleavy

Printed in the USA on acid-free paper.
Order online: www.finishinglinepress.com
 also available on amazon.com

Author inquiries and mail orders:
Finishing Line Press
P. O. Box 1626
Georgetown, Kentucky 40324
U. S. A.

Table of Contents

Pop Rocks 1

Wax Lips 2

Pez 3

Butterfinger 4

Tic Tac 5

Milk Duds 6

Big League Chew 7

Milky Way 8

Life Savers 9

Fog Dancing 10

Big Bend 11

Steel plant orbiting the overpass on I-490 12

Las Nimitas 13

Nighthawks 14

On the child in front of Cordova's Machu Picchu
    after Dark (pa' Victoria Santa Cruz, Makario Sakay,
    y Aaron Dixon) 15

Night Terror 16

Pop Rocks

feel like
when the redbud pods touch the humid tongue of spring
and pop

feel like
the parking lot must when the near perfect cleavage of mica
makes it shimmer

feel like
so many lighters flaming in the lawn seats at the Isle
of Wight.

like
hearing someone call it *pop* when you're lonely in a soda
kind of town

like
your mouth's a pot warming kettle corn for dinner in that
lonely town

or
your brother's Chicago shoulders unlocking the bubble wrap
in your back or the percussion caps calling through
a windy city summer

like
Judas' neck after he jumped from the soft tree to
hang

like
Scrapper Blackwell and vinyl scratching their backs
on sapphire.

Wax Lips

Press your smart mouth to a short fuse
and you can catch a fat, red lip for free.
Lips make out .5% of the body's total surface area—

Which might not be accurate   but it feels right
as lips often do.
The dilemma for you, if you're the sun
bathing type, is that your lips will melt.
So if your mug is a fixer-upper
fill it
like a gore-tex tent.

Just think

of all the shapes a kiss can take

with location, timing, target and stakes.
All of our oxygen escapes us.
Let us talk less
save our breaths
and split one
50/50
in the dark.

Pez

A talisman
        with a lump
in his throat just for you.

You strut
        having captured something
          bright enough
to light a pocket

then one of the troubled
        splits their smoke
and you flip
        Zippos instead.

Butterfinger

There's so much to say when eating peanut butter
and butane. If a cartoon can hush the orange luster
mouth shut, so can you. We're not burning with surprise
at how a big hustle makes us savor the stabilized
oils that run through our rapids. The shelf life
of organic peroxides is less conservative
for candy bars with an alternative
waistline.

What's fatal in five grams is the least damage
I'll hand myself all week. All hours
us poor, man, everyman seeks and steadily devours
white powders spun safe for a head blush like cocaine.
Isn't that something?
Yes, deathless as greed, I abandon
earth-built nourishment grown
green enough to make a mantis jealous,
praying in a lawn of grass blades.

Tic Tac

peppermint cocoon
forgotten in a pocket
shy of mint condition

Milk Duds

As much tool as treat.
Popcorn extractor
and the loose   tooth
goes along for the ride
        and leaves a socket juicy
The executioner would approve

If I believed in prayers,
I'd give the wind my sacraments
   The iron in the blood
would fortify the chocolate—
a new super-alloy
of a stain,
desperate to grab you
by the collar

Big League Chew

Incontrovertibly
born from the spirit of
ballplayers tongue-twisting
jawfuls of Lexington

tillage. The ravings of
countless identical
cheeks like a hoarder's den:
Anthropomorphically

speaking, they're chipmunks with
histories damning them.
'80 was great for the
children of boomers that

boldly washed diamonds in
sweetened expectorate.
Pouches and pouches have
mouth-quaked our childhoods.

Funny how smoking a
candyland cigarette
never got stuck in our
craws like the shredded stuff.

Milky Way

Named after malted milk
not the big bang
by-product now housing
our Saturnalias.

And all the better for it:
Thin scrims of slap-dash caramel.
The weak economy of nougat.

How did we let an edible thing,
bring 1961 the horror
of Buster Keaton on a Billboard
with a singing cow:
There's so much milk in a Milky Way…
You can almost hear it…
Moo.
No you can't.

But now your head is sizzling
with the visual platitudes of artisanal dairy farming
possessed
of less than galactic flavors.

Life Savers

A man invents a five-flavor
        prism riot
by way of Garrettsville, OH
        in 1912—

a summer candy built
        to keep
its composure in a density
        of heats

the man also makes a boy
        not so bent
on composure but of considerable density
        himself

crushed under the weight
        of a bridge
in the shadow
        of The Wasteland,

no rainbow rings or service
        give chase
as the bow of the *Orizaba* gives the Gulf
        a legend.

Fog Dancing

When I learned that fog
was a low-lying cloud,
I ran outside
to move in the sky's
great white geographies.

I called to the crow's ocean
to come down
and meet me in the cinder swells
of Dag Hammarskjöld Elementary's
parking lot.

Because that is my favorite type of sky.
A sky blue like the deep slate
of Lake Erie in March.
Like the umbrage
of Nassau's blue prism arrogance
refracted.

Of course I dance.
I am in the cool white
       before the thermometer gets tall
and turns the harder blocks
into butcher shops.

Of course I dance.
       We tried to kill the river
and it lived.
       We drink its ashes.

We mock the desalination plants.
Our shores born fresh,
the unlocked tonic,
 deep.

Big Bend

No one shouts
when the grandeur's just backdrop.
When the hogbacks and hoodoos
can't hold their own against
that pocket watch.
Do you remember when the intonation
of the hills made them all questions?

I do.
And so I'm here,
west of the Chisos mountains,
to sit before the jazz of javelinas
dancing with the prickly pears.
                It doesn't matter
if the fairy chimneys
send my folklore smoking into the desert
because the elders whisper it to dirt.
When the snake oil finally gives out,
the cartels satellite map the topography,
            and eat the wilderness raw.

We wrap ourselves
        in soft Mexican brandy
because the world has no more
use for gentle men.

Night again,
    prayers climb
        from the Bend's endangered porch lights
to the wall of Rio Grande canyons—
paid for and built
with millions of years.

Steel plant orbiting the overpass on I-490

That building is undeniably

>
> a quantum locked ziggurat moon
> floating from Bocklin's brush.

Down in the ankles
of that hinged phantasm
are the hands
    that once loved
the time clock's grim voltage.

An old man dimming
in a blue nylon bomber jacket

>
> is an abandoned factory dreaming
> of the men that used
> to work inside him.

How brutish and American his medicine—
A poison?
It must taste so—
at least on the tips of
Luxembourghish tongues.

Las Nimitas
>*for Angel*

They must have cleaned out
all of the butchers in Brooklyn
for the stew that night—
seven animals entranced in the stock pot:
young goat, smoked pork bones, chuleta ahumada
and a mystery of others. The hard constitution
of root vegetables softened
with time like an old uncle.

When it's time to learn merengue
        I swoon with rum and your cousins
as they teach me to move and huddle
        around me like a new project.

Later,
we blow out the candles,
and pass those small torches
to the firefly's bellies.
They flicker out into the street
where the shadows are no longer conjecture.
Glow for broke,
protectors of brown bodies.
Let the vigil burn.

Nighthawks

I walked an ephemeral stretch
of Chicago until I found her.

Hiding not so deep
on a second or third floor
was June.
Sitting with her one kid wish
   at respirator rhythm.

      The man that will never be her husband
asks her to sit with him
      beside the beveled edges of the evening.

Read your folded emerald, June.
      The world becomes fluorescent.

On the child in front of Cordova's Machu Picchu After Dark
(pa' Victoria Santa Cruz, Makario Sakay, y Aaron Dixon)

He kneels before the Funk
-blown speakers of the monolith
that once bumped the orphic melody
of Earth, Wind, and Fire.

I watch as his new religion pulls
his thoughts and holds them
as sure and absurd as a lunar tide.

First, it's the lo-fi love of a black-gloved fist
serving a poor child's meal.
Then the stolen thunder of the cajon,
or the long black hair of rebellion
welling in a Philippine jungle.

He kneels
to press his ear to dead speakers,
and drum his fingers
to the beat of a forgotten wattage.

Night Terror

Evening again
and your brain is a pink lantern
                      floating through a thunderhead

      ready as the medicine that winds
your mind like a pocket
watch set for
      dawn

I've always wondered how your day
      gets so rewired in the night
why sleep comes with
      nightmare and seizure
  steeping
in the liquor of your glands

When you kick
                              a dim bulb
stands its ground against the dark

You kick again
      I imagine you dancing
your toes shining
as they rush through the black
volcanic glass of the Umbrian coast
      or drinking from the tiger lilies
      buzzed out and roaring
like the coke-blown club kids of Lyon

      How far away that all feels
from the ancient Hindus placing sleep
on a path
    It is beneficial to lie down with the head placed eastward or southward

I suppose they would call us careless
   in our Cardinal sins
our heads so reckless in direction
   By three a.m. you've surely made it to the shores
     where they inhale
powdered diamond, where their lungs
scintillate like snowbanks in the midnight of their bodies

That's the midnight
   where we will sketch the dream eater
and Baku will swallow your burdens
    Where another fool will write of us
     as stardust
And we'll combust
and the hundred watt shadow
will rest

in the outlets.

Mike Santora earned his MFA in creative writing from the University of New Hampshire. He lives in Cleveland with his wife and daughter. This is his first chapbook.